mur

mur

ation

mur

mur

ation

a.b. dillon

thistledown press

©A.B. Dillon, 2020
All rights reserved

No part of this publication may be reproduced or transmitted in any form or by any means, graphic, electronic or mechanical, including photocopying, recording, or any information storage and retrieval system, without permission in writing from the publisher or a licence from The Canadian Copyright Licensing Agency (Access Copyright). For an Access Copyright licence, visit www.accesscopyright.ca or call toll free to 1-800-893-5777.

Thistledown Press Ltd.
410 2nd Avenue North
Saskatoon, Saskatchewan, S7K 2C3
www.thistledownpress.com

Library and Archives Canada Cataloguing in Publication

Title: Murmuration / A.B. Dillon.
Other titles: Mur mur ation
Names: Dillon, A. B., 1968- author.
Description: Poems.
Identifiers: Canadiana 20200280821 | ISBN 9781771871976 (softcover)
Classification: LCC PS8607.I458 M87 2020 | DDC C811/.6—dc23

Author photograph by Grace Dillon
Cover and book design by Jackie Forrie
Printed and bound in Canada

Canada Council
for the Arts
Conseil des Arts
du Canada

Thistledown Press gratefully acknowledges the financial assistance of the Canada Council for the Arts, SK Arts, and the Government of Canada for its publishing program.

Acknowledgements

I gratefully acknowledge my inner circle, who have supported me during the writing of this book, in particular Lyndon Penner, Kelly Shepherd and Andy Moro. Thanks also to Thistledown Press for your kind attention.

Many thanks must go to my editor, Seán Virgo, whose friendship and guidance has meant so much to me. My love and affection to you, Seán. I treasure working with you.

To my children, Grace and Callaghan, I am in debt to you both for allowing me great swaths of time in solitude in order to write. Every cup of tea and every hug has meant the world. This book exists because of your selflessness.

To the Pen Cap King, thank you for believing in this book, for your patience and love. Your constancy has been my compass.

For the boy who ran through fields of daisies.

I am

Having trouble

Breathe

choking

I love
you
+ you

It is hard to Breath

Pain

Is my bladder
Cathe

feels like my bladder

is not emptying.

CONTENTS

SEPARATION

ALIGNMENT

COHESION

it is curious to Us
this, your unseeing murmur nation
— Crow

In murmuration, each bird is aware of the seven nearest to itself, following three basic principles while in flight: separation, alignment and cohesion.

I began to
think about
sevens.

SEPARATION

1.

Spying

I don't remember you without the scars.

Hugging you wasn't for solace, it was a reconnaissance mission.
I needed information. Pressing my ear against your chest, I spied
on the enemy.

I knew your heart.
It was a timebomb in a cage.

I knew the waves in your hair, which I studied every Sunday from
the back seat of the car on the way to Mass. I knew the feel of the
inside of your wrist when you'd take your watch off, trailing my
index finger over the divets.

When your lips went pale, I knew the enemy was winning.

There isn't much difference between a brink or a frontier where
existence is concerned. You did so much at the brink of life.

I hover here, inhabiting this threshold world of in between mo-
ments, taking comfort in the silence on either side of a heartbeat,
or the holiness of water trapped in a plastic bubble, in a prayer
card from Lourdes.

 lub dub lub dub

            lub dub

                        lub

2.

Assimilation

you grew ivy on our house in Ontario,
which had the look of an Irish seancéal,
distinct and ancient

to my mind, made us the envy
of the street

I used to circle round and pull my hand through the leaves,
summer to autumn, emerald to vermillion

inside, things were less covetous

our gold velvet sofa and chair
and the vulgar red carpet

a brass fireplace fender and coal scuttle from the old country
rendered useless

a holy water font at the front door
crucifixes hung over thresholds
so familiar as to go unnoticed

after some years,
you pulled the ivy down
concerned about the state of the brick underneath

you pulled it all down

3.

Remnants

things not quite used,
nor discarded:

unsorted photographs
in a drawer in the kitchen

a rusted horseshoe nailed under the basement stairs
to keep our luck from running out

a brass spoon belonging to your mother
which should have been hung on a rack

but never was

4.

Ascending, Descending

you are lying on the sofa
when I come home from school

your face is weary
and I am shy to see you so prone and uncertain,

My brother's died you say,
He's gone and died

and the best I can offer .
is a cold compress
which you accept, like a child
and for the first time I see the illusion

we are in an Escher stairwell

ascending or descending, no matter;

inwardly, inwardly
perception has bent my world
like a spoon

5.

Summoned

children were dispatched like carrier pigeons
to deliver the message

and the summoned made their way up to Farrelly's
for the phone

voices were raised just shy of a shout
and between hollered exchanges, there were lags

pauses for tin-canned words to open
on the other side of the sea

we gathered around the table,
straining to hear what your face was saying

6.

Resonance

My father could pull a plough
you used to say

Like a giant he was, with a chest this broad —
your two arms spread wide, to show me

and I'd imagine this colossus of a man
working the field in the rain
calling to his Gypsy Cob mare as the old ridging plough
cut furrows through the heavy soil

From that sodden field in Armagh,
consciousness disseminates from him to you and to me

to quark through my hands like premonitions
into the clay loam of my garden

all of us are labouring —
he in his field under the soft, good rain
you, pulling the ivy down off the grey brick
and me, under the lambent prairie sun, considering the lilies

I felt sorrowly for the horse
whose name I would never know

7.

On One Hand

Father

Athair

we speak in the garden,
you from invisible otherwheres,
me digging in the soil

and I ask you things like

What should I do or
How can I possibly cope?

I can count on one hand the things you said to me
that I could apply to this world —

No one ever said it was going to be easy.

Do you think he has it in him to do that, love?

Your mother means well.

Remember why you left.

if only you poorlies would allow Us
to land upon your shy and careful chests

then, unlock yourselves
open-ribbed to let your feelings
fly upwardly,

We could carry the sorrows away

indeed, do you not know
how devoted We are to wing you to empty?

— Corro

1.

Unfurling

I don't really know
which varieties of plants will thrive together,

if it's crowding in or generosity of space
that makes safely
the green push

At the planting
is hope

for the unfurling
of upwardly leafy faces toward their gods

as they commit seppuku

I have my regrets in verdant spaces.

2.

Scumbling

I garden by colour, painterly,
and by feel

this violet thrums the right frequency
against the van Gogh mustardly riverstrokes behind

and that Matisse blue is an aria,

scumbling like an afterthought swipe of mooncool
through the persimmon, which splays its fiery
sun fingers on a duskhard lake

the humming of chroma, lightfasting side by each
is a palette of bees in a huehive

3.

Bare Feet

dark half moons of soil packed under my nails
wet cold,
and damp with promise

the weight of me sinking into
pennybrown vale

gardening calls for a red cotton dress
and bare feet

a wide brimmed sun hat
made from straw

a slug loiters on the sepals
of a white starflower

4.

Scarlet

everything used to be like gardening

so much of my life chosen
by feel;

what conclusions might be inferred
from the blush upon my cheek,

pinpricked scarlet

while kneeling at Mass?

5.

Critique

the tiger lillies are crowded
and there is too much orange,
the palette is off, caustic

(this is what happens
when I go by feel)

my feel
is a chamber consort
that has lost tempo

6.

And Other Miracle Cures

Cennini's handbook for Renaissance artists
could be shelved in the self-help section of any bookstore

learn how to prep a surface for a painting
or mend a broken heart

discern which bones are best
and the manner in which to burn them

grind them into a fine powder
and combine saliva with this dust to prime

lick your wounds;
spittle upon the eyes to see, in the ears to hear

to cure — forgive them, they do not know your paradise

Ephphatha

be opened

you peoples are tending to look to the light, erstwhile.
Us is of a grand black symphysis,
absorbing all,
drinking light unto itself, behold,
as bendish blues and dappledown greens
stay hidden in aftervanes,
and soil soakens up sunbeams

We delight in our blueblack Onemind kuu,
specially for secrets and hopes,
for noble wishes and for all manner of wanhope

— Karasu

7.

Awakening

what must push upwardly
out of purpletinged desire

ochresinned scarlet
soaked to bursting

this colloquy

is the fathomless green swell

thus it is said
amongst
We

as the crow flies

do you not know

the path forward
is not in your eyes

thusly We flee,

thusly
We
fly

darkly we know
where the light is

— Cuervo

1.

Grandmother Praying

the beads knock against the pew
as you murmur the rosary

our lady of the stars
stands on a snake, and I feel afraid
that she isn't afraid

while you whisper
I search your eyes for the truth
as you look upon your lady
of the stars,

your lady
of seven sorrows

2.

Pinning

faintly, at the closeness of our faces,
your breath hinted of tea, sweetly so

there was intimacy in this work,
far more touch than would otherwise allow

I remember the feel of your knuckle
pressing in to the hollow of my back,
heel toe heel toe, from sacrum
to the nape of my neck

and the feel of pins
scratching at the backs of my knees

3.
Still

all your considerations
were mine to wear

there were petticoats and knitted vests
to protect me from maladies

like wind around your heart, for instance, or the pleurisy

you'd look over the rim of your glasses, like God
and hum through pin-clamped lips

Stand still, child dear.
My dere chylde.

4.

Signs

nightly, the sign of the cross
your brambled hand over mine
teaching the correct order

in the name of the father and of the son
and of the holy ghost

you'd leave me to sleep like a recumbent effigy
hands folded at my heart

wondering why the Lord would ever take my soul
to keep

5.

After His Funeral

I'm trying for to tell you that her daddy died —

you say to the nurse, who fusses with the diaper, prattling on,
your brogue still too thick
despite all the years in Montréal

your mouth is a grotto; you are ignored

I sit in funeral garb in the corner of your bedroom

you hadn't sewn the dress I had worn

it was empty of words

she is full of raucous laughters
her face all lit up and wonderous

I make a swoop overtoppen her
like a benediccioun

— Kraii

6.

Bespoken

When my body belonged to the two of us,
before anyone else's opinions stung, before the perception
that I wasn't enough
I slipped the dress you'd made over my head
and stepped out into the world clothed in love

bespoken

Things I remember:

Your powder blue suitcase with the Via Rail tag on the handle.
Your boiled lambs' wool coat, the colour of a black poodle, with a
fur collar and a hat to match, the pockets of which were like velvet
galaxies to explore, which you tolerated during Mass. The occa-
sional Kraft caramel waited inside.

Your stout legs, varicose veined, compressed in hosiery that
would squeeze the life out of a lesser mortal. Your girdles, which
we made merciless fun of, and how hard you laughed, even
though to do so was well beneath your station.

The ache of the silence when you left me. There was no laughter
at the dinner table, no one to require decent conversation once
you'd gone, no one to talk about the lovely roast or the beautiful
gravy. The loss of lovely, the disappearance of beautiful.

What it was like to wait for your parcel to come from Montréal,
done up in brown paper and tied expertly with twine, as though
the war was still on.

7.

Lowering

wishing for the old ways —

the dead laid out on the table,
the house filled with the knowing and the known;

the banter, the hum to the hush of it,
giving way to vigil

the lowering of the heart into the well
before the cobbled walk to earthsoaked womb

Go you to bed, love, and have a good wee lie down

Your glasses folded on top of the bedside table,
and your handkerchief tucked up the sleeve
of your nightgown,

the one you'd embroidered with sweet peas

I'm after hearing your boyo vivaldi
asinging dolorosa hymnnims through the window
which she leaves open of a morning

> *eia, mater, fons amoris*
> *me sentire vim doloris*
> *fac, ut tecum lugeam*

calling for her mamakind

— Kråke

1.

Cellular

pockets are strange accomplices nowadays,
dialing whenever they feel the compulsion

pockets used to have nothing to do
with ruination

there used to be a rotary dial to slow the hand,
and a cord to keep us safely tethered
to a wall or inside a box

free of its restraints, the phone pings
as it passes by the towers
in this new Babel

while you went about your business, your pocket
had other ideas

of course you are blameless,

like spare change and lint
are blameless

2.

The Flood

the Bow had become swollen
near to breaking Herself open

you had moved on up the hill
and I had stayed in the house
by the River

it felt parabolic to have remained here

standing in the stairwell at the window
as the River was speaking to me
about my foolish choices

yet I was compelled
to walk by Her banks daily,
among strangers who wore skyward apocryphal faces
like Hieronymous studies

on the path, a wet pink baby's shoe
without its mate

all the birds had gone silent

3.
Risen

River tried to teach me
about the bedlam of
Her current

and how I had long suppressed
my own raging nature

here She came, rising
by the hour,

as if to say
that She would swallow me whole

4.

Not Quite Returning

a white X was used during the plague
but I made mine out of green painter's tape
marked my front door,
became an evacuee

taking refuge in your house
on the hill, sleeping on the sofa beneath you

a voyeur of the parallel universe version
of who we could have been

at night, thundering kawelit skies
Our throatie exhaultations
serenade the great darkness

Our silences, thereabounds,
makes the moon loudly bryht in heofon
in seventhheavenish

when you go silent
you can sing the rain

— Coroune

5.

Return

after three days, River calms
it is time to return to my house by the River
and face the sodden

solitary

there is
a stillpoint with you
an embrace in your hallway
and for that moment,

a neither here nor there —
not having left nor remained

then,
like a dunkard, a lapsi

falling backward
into the water

6.

What I Wonder

Do you wish so deeply, though?
for those moments
when we were wide open
like children's faces at the new
and we tried so earnestly
for landing
surely

the stairwell

and the sound of her little feet thereupon,

descending

7.

Or is it what is repudiated, what must be denied
for penance, because of the heart's atrocities?

the search for atonement
with every beating thought of it

in flying
keep close to the sky

in singing
keep close to the sound

abranch or awire
think of the circle
feel the humthrum of the current

to become part of the one blackish line in parelement
let the wind
know the feather

— Krahe

ALIGNMENT

1 pearlie
9 buttons
6 shells
12 prettypretty china bits
4 tinnies
7 wee sharp bones
5 glassies
1 ring for the ear
4 tags
3 hooks
6 danglies
8 shiny pebbles

She holds the pearl in her hand,
and this does sit me well and high abranch.

— Kuroo

1.

Life Drawing

the forgotten sound of conte
pulled against the teeth of Fabriano paper

the rasp of a thin charcoal stick
which cries out when caught correctly, on its edge

his belly rises and falls like a sleeping child's

2.

Pause

there is a painting in the Uffizi
of a happy boy clutching
a goldfinch

bello e grasso
beautiful and fat
child of a Medici

I pause
at this painting

because the boy is full of joy
and the bird is suffering

3.

Studio

at work, the figure emerges easily
and I am as much a witness
as any other dumbstruck buffoon

I am outside of my body,
up and away,

oddly similar to the witnessing
of one's own assault

(another kind
of bird's eye view)

when my blewe eyes
had not yet turned to black

and my beak-red skin told the tale
of short days lived

my sweet yumyum mamakind
croaked reedily unto me
sweetily unto me

— Kráka

4.

Red, Blue

and I think about him beneath me
how it would feel to subsume

this cerulean red
like war paint on my breasts

and on his face,
lapis lazuli

5.

Passage

he sculpts me on a Sunday

(this is my green secret)

pulled up and through the grey stem
from the root
toward an outrageous metanoia

and still, I decide,

death and rebirth
must be better than living

6.

Blinded

cruelty becomes a feast to gorge upon,
the infliction of it

a benevolence

as on the battlefield,
crows pluck the eyes from dead soldiers

to feed to their young

7.

Memento Mori

flowers wrapped in plastic
left on the countertop to wilt

or petals
falling to the earth

both are a kind of offering;

the former
is also a statement

of another kind of death

well now, your lot knows that one is for sorrow
as the singsong rhymebellis rings

so shall it be
softeli oon
sorrowly won

— Sorrë

1.

Mother

arriving at night to Fethard on Sea,
we climb the stairs
and slide open the door to the balcony

Standing in silence,

we cannot tell black water
from black sky

we are folded in the wings
of a great, obsidian Crow

2.

Tidal

there is something childlike about you,
your hand searching for mine

the stars are deafening

I ponder the blacks of west Indian peas
and berries of atropa belladonna

we surrender to the walloping silence
of the sky

pulling upward

inward

brought her two shiny tidbitties of glass this day
from the edges of the bended river
where Our bow reedies grow

her face, the tale I am loving to read
speakens of silent thinkings and musings and allsorts

— Kaw'qs

3.

A Moment

here is love,

your hand warm in mine,
familiar and modest

4.

Two Wishes

you see a shooting star
and tell me of a childhood wish
that has just come true;

the sea and the stars
have made us quiet
and small

I sense a shift within you —
not quite surrender, but a decision

it feels like you're resolved
now,

to go

5.

Whereas I wish
for you to remain

substantial,

distinct against all planes,
attainable

I close my eyes
and
vault a prayer

into the terrible black dome

6.

that you might safely journey,
slán abhaile,
safe home

near you, but for now

skyward,
you're smiling

7.

and I'm a mutinous daughter
resenting the falling star,
while you delight

wishes
are
cold
things

COHESION

Variation: One

and I know it makes no simple sense
holy water in plastic bubbles

I have my regrets

she stands on a snake unafraid
enclosed in the wings
of a great obsidian crow

I had forgotten the sound
which cries out

when caught correctly

indeed every wind has known my feathers
and though I am hollow
I am full

— Corb

Variation: Two

all of us digging
and burning the bones

your breath smells sweet,
reminding us

all the birds were silent and
we tried to take in the deafening stars

there was something childlike about you
pulling upward and inward

a feeling

Variation: Three

I was shy to see you this way,
prone through the divinely pulled

recumbent effigy

as if by dream,
the figure emerges

a real time witness
as any other,

dumbstruck

Variation: Four

you were aware
the raising of voices just shy of a shout

damp with promise,

the weight of me, sinking

stand still

lick at lapis

swallow

Variation: Five

except for Sundays, my whole life was chosen

trying to imprint the memory

vault a prayer
into the terrible

Variation: Six

How can I possibly cope?

No one ever said it was going to be easy.

(This is what happens
when I go by feel.)

I knew there'd be no laughter

it was wartime,

and we tried so earnestly
descending among the things, unready

cruelty to gorge upon,
rapturous

Variation: Seven

I pulled my hands through
the gold purpletinged desire

the hum of it,
the hush

I resent;
you delight

like petals falling

Miss Mercy

Miss Mercy is divine in Ours.

We see her tending to you lot extra much.
She is of kindnesses and clemencies,
smallish downy deeds.
Her shyabouts and hidings We keen to.

Miss Mercy is singsong the livelongday,
good morning starshine, the earth says hellooooo!

She is our starshine lady, to be true . . .

and Us,

Us is her hidden parlement of the wire,
the lamppost, the rooftop murder,

and the worshipshop, lo!

of a Sunnandæġ

where you lot gather
to click and clap and go tellit on the mow-un-tin
overthehills andeveree wher-ruh!

We are about spying our divinest starsong maiden
while she is bringen extra foodstuffs to her sadsmile bencher.
He lufe so deeply his Miss Mercy,

yes ma'am, very much yassss!

Her sees this lufum boyo as a saintly so and so,
the bench as his throne, lo,
and the liquid he sources in the flask for his happies,
well, Miss Mercy pays no nevermind.

We hear hims reedily murmur that her is

bee

yuu

tifull

and spy his gringrinface lookin like a weeboy,
his dewgrey eyes soft upon her, his sweetsoft ladylovedove.

She laughs and cracks
when he makes his warbles for her.

For this, We drop many rich gifties,
foil bits and shiny glass, trinkets
and bendyBow treasures.

Someofa times, Miss Mercy stoops
to keep pocketwise Our bestowals,
which does dandy please Us so dreadful much
that we raucous cawlit and crouken
a big blackish thunder.

the boyo knows,
he hears Us, lying
kingly abench among you,
a Pitticus sage, unseen.

Ergo, We call him our brotherbird,
and welcome his soft spiritus among Us
to fly,

a treetop
a skyblast

to be looken down upon the bendyBow and remember,
before the unkindness,
before alonement and sorrowly,

when you winged in felicitatem,
in syllaba with Us,

where Our reedies
grew.

Miss Mercy is oft about sayen

Yuh bruk fi mi heart!

to the sadsmile boyoKing,

and she crack and crack at them toothless gringrins
he gives unto her,
like a newjoy tiny gives unto his most beloved mamakind.

Oft, I perch abench for spying purposes,
or to warn her of impendings
She of a time comes over and holds out a crust,
for even I Miss Mercy wants to loveadoveup.

She is no trickster, but a soft yumyum maiden, mind you,
and she says unto me
she says —

Yuh g'wine do it?
Yuh g'wine tek de treat yuh big black crah?

And yes,
yes yessireebobbeee!

I do take the treat,
I take the crusty breadbit, and offer unto her
thricelythree hearty croaks, lo!

Because if you can't nyam the bread from the hand of Mercy,
then you deserve to go hungry, methinks.

so it is with feelings
that come to perch upon the heart

open the chestcage wide
for spacey freedoms

nothing stays

which is as it should be,
foreverandever, ahhmymen

hollow out your
heart flute

like the komuso
play their shakuhachi

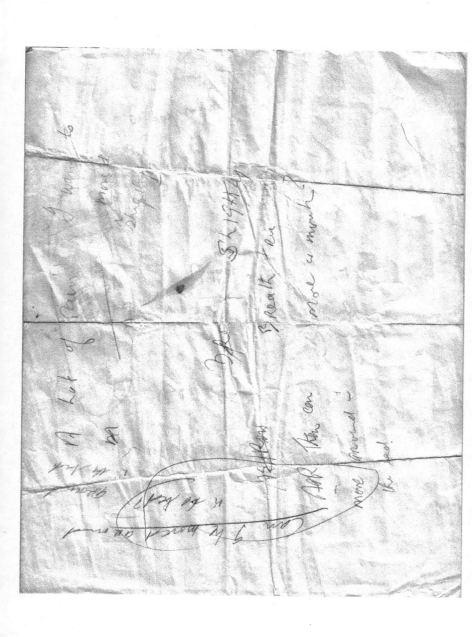

Fugue

Do you remember how I'd be the first to find the National Geographic in the mailbox?

Yes, you were a wee thief

I was so sad to look at the whales being slaughtered, men in gum boots knee deep in blood.

You couldn't have known how the world could be cruel

And I never told you.

No, you never did

a lot of pain
it is hard to breathe

but then, the stars . . .

there was another boyoKing, once upon a timely
you lot thought him a nutter,
but Us called him a Brotherbird

he painted wheatfield with crows, you know it?

you cannot decide
do the crows fly away or toward?

palendromie sillinesses

Us is of riotous laughter, murmurnation
We love a good riddledeedee

the turbulent spirally dance,
the luminant lovedove swirl,
he danced there,
in what you call a madness

what We call

extasie

all of us digging
burning the bones
saintly so-and-so's

pay no nevermind,
murmurnation

effigies, undertows,

eternal sleep
move just slightly

laugh

promise,
there are *sages* to see

stand still

please go on
take the crust

no one ever said
you can't take

from the hand of mercy

my ahhmens,
pull your tiny hands through your purpletinged desires
let it land softly

like seven petals falling

nothing stays

yes I did my verybest yes humble
placation of lowering my head and turning
just so yes to present her with
the flower of mine eye unblinkingly full
of blackish prayers and methinks she has
put twoandtwotogether and yes knows it is
mountainme from the sea come to be
yes sweet message me yes there is
nothing like firsterly lovedove yes which is
an unction upon an unbeating suddenly beating
yes